CW01498154

IN ME THE JUNCTURE

Nisha Ramayya

'I say that Relation is made up of all the differences in the world and that we shouldn't forget a single one of them, even the smallest.'

Édouard Glissant

SAD PRESS

978-1-912802-28-9

BRISTOL 2019

Containing Passages from Dictionaries;
Along with the Shell or Husk;
Along with the Membrane

this is the shell of the mundane egg
winding from left to right
appearing outside itself
life and heart appear outside itself

you have 'not seen before'
turning from left to right
opening to the right
the valve of which opens to the right

a bivalve shell
(moving slowly)
an elephant's head
(difficult penance)
anything shaped like a cauldron

she is 'lotus-born'
world blooms from her navel
crusted whorls soften in salt

her staircase body
crawls out of its shell
formed like a palace or temple

three lines in the neck
(marking good fortune)
shell-necked tortoise
unanswerable lines

your neck folds like a spiral shell
wounds caused by finger nails
working after pearls

she wears bracelets of gold and shell
the shell of anything
blows into battle-white
sheath of pleasure
sheath of will or life

the convolution of a shell
jewel-studded evening hour
sea-flower pearl-shell
she husks herself loudly

your hair curls to the right
(she is an auspicious mark)
ashes of burnt shell
shell-born and shell-dissolver
drink the impossible milk

stupid, a kind of bracelet

She is made of pale red, pink, pallid, or forming part of it, these are specific smiles. We stand on white bed sheets and tinfoil, a layer of sacred grass spread out at a sacrifice, she sits where the fire can reach her. Bound to the ground, a house-hero, carpet-knight, the pejorative feminine is unnecessary.

The jumping shapes of the painted elephant, the human-faced eagle, the white horse, the music that follows him. Sister failure pushing the reflection into her making her small, a pale red hue, rose colour.

This relates to the *patali*, or trumpet flower, which you place in every hole, you must hear each part. She is quiet and still while she waits, her other rolled under the sheets, the corpsy-lumps of a body wrapped in cheap cloth. Thirty-six hours later trimmings and tearings as soft as the sound of finger finding thumb.

Words pierce (half prose half verse): she's never looked more beautiful, or, it's all downhill from here.

Many of these definitions mention claws falling off, a temporary symptom associated with the worm (pernicious to hair, nails, and teeth). Transcription of an old woman's mumble [after marriage everything stops].

Zooming into her skin so close the petals appear, her face is frilled and bearing. They write songs about this, filling tips and tongues in the well of nectar of poetry; I dip mine in disease.

A species of rice ripening in the rains, they cut her knuckles forcing the love up her arms. It can be beautiful, the side glance expressing, the rays of the ascending sun, her written skin.

The act of cutting or dividing or cutting off or mutilating (with teeth or nails), tracing her spine to mark the line she has crossed.

Of an artificial poem, crying, proclaiming, a decidedly subjective title.

Who can remember how many steps the ritual requires, the foot as a measure of length, forming the end, final.

Awkward Bumping in the Theory District

In losing halves, the materiality of the reading experience mediates the sincerity of your voice. 'Make three true "we" statements each': longing, not releasing between-whiles.

I read poetry to drink with imaginary friends.

Transferring the investment unkind, from mountain to cry. The plan believes itself to be special, having been assured of its specialness since birth.

The feeling that takes soundings and scrapes, aims, and knock-down blows us. Reduced to an equality, my jokes become funnier.

I read poetry to maintain my honour.

The loose tangles of habit and taste (an annotated bibliography). Thinking of ourselves as more than distance corrects the attachment.

In the time it took me to retrieve my cards, the connection imperative became a stylised refusal.

Don't take the mutual response personally, a success story.

We can do more than run circles around the subject: brown eyes, blue eyes, two thirds into the first day.

I tear my way through getting to know you (the half-life reasserts itself wholefully). Not politicised, not finding my people, frowning to hear the question asked.

The unnatural ease of disentanglement. Unhappily having, to spend time writing one thing instead of another.

Works are what you say: stop before tumbling. Grace as the ways we might fit.

Secretions or Obstructions

1

You come too late, much too late. There will always be a world – a white world – between you and us.... The other's total inability to liquidate the past once and for all. In the face of this affective ankylosis of the white man, it is understandable that I could have made up my mind to utter my Negro cry. Little by little, putting out pseudopodia here and there, I secreted a race. (Fanon 2008: 92)

2

In the face of this affective 'formation of a stiff joint by consolidation of the articulating surfaces' –

In the face of this affective 'coalescence of two bones originally distinct' –

It is understandable that I, like a critical rub, could have the advantage of taking into your skin and the disadvantage of going off.

You come too late, embarrassed by the analogy between you and us. You say what doesn't come to mind: 'toasted bread or potatoes, peat, lignite, withered leaves'.

You say the utterly in common.

There will always be a world in which this self, projecting inwards or outwards, separates.

Likeness to likeness, we are marrow-scooped in the face of the articulating surfaces. Chins pointing down to the drops of oil in backlit water, we give ourselves away.

3

In *On Being Included: Racism and Diversity in Institutional Life*, Sara
Ahmed considers the arrival of the stranger in the university (she discusses
the implicit racialisation of the stranger elsewhere). In the institutional space,
the body of colour is, statistically and otherwise, the body out of place.
Reflecting on her experiences of working in British and Australian
universities, Ahmed writes: 'When an arrival is noticeable, we notice what is
around. I look around and re-encounter the sea of whiteness. I had become
so used to this whiteness that I had stopped noticing it' (2012: 35). This
impression of whiteness is an impression of coherence that results from a
gathering of white bodies; the body of colour disrupts this coherence:

> It is important to remember that whiteness is not reducible to white
> skin or even to something we can have or be, even if we pass through
> whiteness. When we talk about a 'sea of whiteness' or 'white space,' we
> talk about the repetition of the passing by of some bodies and not
> others. And yet non-white bodies do inhabit white spaces; we know
> this. Such bodies are made invisible when spaces appear white, at the
> same time as they become hypervisible when they do not pass, which
> means they 'stand out' and 'stand apart.' You learn to fade in the
> background, but sometimes you can't or you don't. (42)

The stranger who wishes to pass – whom Ahmed describes as 'the "right
kind" of minority, the one who aims not to cause unhappiness or
trouble' (157) – tries not to stand out. She minimises her difference in an
attempt to blend into the surroundings, to reproduce the coherence of the
white space by blending, by fading, by dissolution.

Standing out is the cause and effect of uncomfortable feelings. The stranger
does not like to sit down, for fear that she will be asked to leave. She does
not like to make herself comfortable, for fear that she has misheard the
invitation:

> Whiteness is produced as host, as that which is already in place or at
> home. To be welcomed is to be positioned as the one who is not at
> home. Conditional hospitality is when you are welcomed on condition
> that you give something back in return. (43)

What may be given back in return? What may be given in order to return?
The intensity of the stranger's gratitude corresponds to the impact of her
returns.

4

Frantz Fanon suggests that whiteness is rigidity, brittle coalescence; blackness is projection, extraction, supersaturated release. Ahmed's rendering of the body of colour is similarly obtrusive – a cluster of sore points, swellings and stains. Although the 'sea of whiteness' implies fluidity, the body of colour may experience the continuous body of whiteness as an obstruction ('like banging your head against a brick wall'):

> Things might appear fluid if you are going the way things are flowing. When you are not going that way, you experience a flow *as* solidity, as what you come up against. In turn, those who are not going the way things are flowing are experienced *as* obstructing the flow. (2012: 186-187)

To come: the incoherence of our bodies is what we bring up, the condition of what we have to bring.

To come up: despite the insufficiencies of the conditions, we don't know when to leave.

To come up against: (the impression of) settling deeply.

5

Kidney stones come to mind.

The stones that pass through the body, leaving the body unchanged.

The stones that must be shattered: they are broken, the body is left unchanged. The stones that must be surgically treated: the body is opened, they leave unchanged.

The mass inside you that resists encouragement, that refuses the slip of the spontaneous passage.

Sometimes obstinacy manifests as inertia, which is an apparently neutral position. It feels as if your body has not caught up to the world; it feels as if the world has not caught up to your body.

Disinclination comes up against the fear of not being missed.

6

There are things that would delete
themselves if only you would let them, damage

to the circulation, and that is what I wanted.
Was a gasped voice from the beginning,

overly phlegmatic, striated to perfection,
the colour of our facets and we wouldn't be

blind. And I could hold myself within me
so tight that I might burst; prolapse of the

epidermis – is that you, polymorphous pervert,
moaning, ah, fuck me in the plural. (Uziell 2016: 4)

7

There are bodies that would dissolve, that would not be contingent upon
the argument of their embodiment. There are arguments that would admit
points to the point of atrophy.

In moving round desires, we go from death to death: 'But the advantage of
syncope is precisely that one always returns from it. Asthmatics, epileptics,
lovers – they recount explicitly how wonderful it is to breathe after the
attack. [...] We place ourselves in the *before* death, in the *after* death. The
real crossing is forgotten' (Clément 1994: 15). The inability to speak
precedes asphyxiation; there is no question apart from the question of who
comes first.

The destroyer of strength said: 'It is built up with bones, smeared over with
flesh, covered with skin, filled with faeces, urine, bile, phlegm, marrow, fat,
grease and also with many diseases, like a treasure house full of wealth'
(Radhakrishnan 1989: 807). I am full of fullness.

The destroyer of strength said: 'In such a world as this, what is the good of
the enjoyment of desires?' (797). My eyes are full of fullness.

Over-identifying with you, I am unable to speak or listen or respond to you. Compressed by the fullness of bodies, my body implodes. (Inertia may manifest as love.)

The argument is hypertrophic, admitting too many colours and consistencies. My desires are irreducible to the point.

8

बिन्दु **bindu**, a detached particle, drop, globule; a pearl; a drop of water taken as a measure; a spot or mark of coloured paint on the body of an elephant; the dot over a letter representing the *anusvāra* [after-sound] (supposed to be connected with Śiva and of great mystical importance); a zero or cypher (in manuscripts put over an erased word to show that it ought not to be erased); a mark made by the teeth of a lover on the lips

9

Orgasm is therefore the foremost means of attaining the dissolution of the individual subject, who thereby becomes the Absolute I, the Immense Heart, or a Forbidden Word. This notion of favouring the moment of syncope is pushed to its extreme consequences; it is true that afterward nothing of value remains. Not sex, nor death, incest, excrement, urine, or even God: it's all the same, or rather, it's All One. (Clément 1994: 139)

10

I light fires in your stomach to worship the tiger eye in your eyes.

The body becomes rancid in the warmth of the embrace.

I absorb your inability, in me the juncture is hardened in fire.

I absorb your inability, in me the hardness reaches extinction.

I absorb the world between you and us, in me the white world reaches extinction.

The body comes into the world, continues into the world, dissolves into the world.

'Thereafter it burns the world, devoid of lustre, devoid of limit, devoid of appearance. It burns the *mahat tattva* : it burns the Unmanifested. It burns the Imperishable. It burns Death' (Radhakrishnan 1989: 890).

In the deadness of night, our eyes filled with slime –

Tell us the great secret of aloneness –

Likeness to likeness, we are utterly fucked.

Responses to a Question about Citation

'I go to libraries because they are the ocean.' I go to the dictionary because these
*
worlds are my world. An impression on each of the four doors 'of the old new

ooh ooh and the old', ah you're shivering ah come inside. You sound like him, has

anyone ever told you that you sound like him. What am I thinking of, anxiety.

A depression on the heart in the shape of a raincloud. What am I thinking of,

anxiety. An impression of the old new 'feels swept away'. I'm laughing, like ah
*
this is too easy; you're laughing, like 'mourning which has already occurred'.

Perhaps I sat on your grave in a previous life, perhaps it was the sitting contented

me. Count me in to the feeling of full of care. The 'fear of a danger' held in

common ('I don't believe in personal property'). The sentimentally aimless

held in community ('my thoughts are not my own'). The 'long secret road / of
*
hiding, surge and observation' (what do you want, I give you what you want).

Why am I going, held by 'imaginary chains' ('I [don't] have the key and I keep

it'). From the base of my spine ('the very origin of love') to the repeated ends of

('the agitation of the universe' is the 'pull my hair' is the 'ah'). 'The candidate's

citational practice is also interestingly inconsistent.' I'm sharing, like it's already
*
lost; the beat is falling, like losing is the fullness we are anxious to regain.

Poetry sounds like: 'the echo anticipate, the hard / bloom underbreath, the

album / eruption'. Poetry sounds like the echo ('an absent lover')

anticipates, the birds return to the caves in your body, a chorus of openings.

Ah come inside 'to move – that is, to fuse spiritually – in the inner space or

sky, the heart, the central void (*kha*) of consciousness' ah your distractions.

Imitating she who vomits the universe, my emptiness consumes action with

fire. She uncoils herself; she is again coiled. 'Crisis is a Hair' in a previous

life, ah the key was tuned down for you. What do you want, the world loses

consciousness. Our shared histories suggest a bristling that becomes a

coming on edge, 'an injury', 'an abandonment', 'a revulsion'. Anxiety is a

supramaterial ascension of the transducing systems, it is that which turns

the petals, 'whose nature is all bliss'. She uncoils herself; you see yourself

reflected in the eyes of the snake. The offering is occasioned by carelessness.

These sleeping worlds are awake to 'existence (regarded as the common property of all things)'. The momentary union of 'it's a little alone, it's a little alone' ah the momentary bliss. 'A partial arising', like the bondage of anxiety ('Past which forces retrograde / If it come in sleep'). An impartial arousal, void of aim, void of the heart opens into the universe. The emptiness between us 'shines like a chain of lights'. Staying with the emptiness between us is ah directionless love ah quiescence. Sometime before the three squares, 'literature is held in common', sometime after the three circles. Ah to draw back from the beloved object, ah 'It – may jolt the Hand / That adjusts the Hair / That secures Eternity'. Ah it's void for you.

Barthes, Roland, *A Lover's Discourse: Fragments*, trans. by Richard Howard (London: Vintage Books, 2002)

Dickinson, Emily, *The Complete Poems*, ed. by Thomas H. Johnson (London: Faber and Faber, 1986)

Greenwell, Bonnie, *Energies of Transformation: A Guide to the Kundalini Process* (Delhi: Motilal Banarsidass, 2002)

Howe, Susan, *My Emily Dickinson* (Berkley: North Atlantic Books, 1985)

Monier-Williams, *A Sanskrit-English Dictionary: Etymologically and Philologically Arranged with Special Reference to Cognate Indo-European Languages* (New Delhi: Asian Educational Services, 2008)

Moten, Fred, *B Jenkins* (Durham: Duke University Press, 2010)

Padoux, André, and Jeanty, Roger-Orphé, *The Heart of the Yoginī: The Yoginīhṛdaya, a Sanskrit Tantric Treatise* (Oxford: Oxford University Press, 2013)

Woodroffe, John, *Shakti and Shakta: Essays and Addresses on the Shakta Tantrashastra* (Charleston: BiblioBazaar, 2008)

Thank You Poem for Robert Hampson

to know by heart
lives between – clarity and 'foreignness'

protect against familiar
here (the Sword personified) – here (a teacher's mouth)

do you have a sense of – logic
do you need to go this far – behind resting

the same teacher – and – the same teacher – and
guided by ammonite

your uncommonly – being – entirely absorbed
this is very simple

moving – in common – because of simplicity
allaying spirals – over in safe – good

consider straight-footed – bare-footed
surpass indefatigable

clear – the breathing present
shelter – the weight at the end of a thread

to approach – asking
means of – yours

Review of Hannah Black's *Some Context*
(Chisenhale Gallery, 2017)

This is a movement from a singular definite to a plural indefinite. The clear meaning understood from the context is 'what is we', 'what is us', 'what is ours'. This meaning is derived from the object of thought – some soft toys – from which many readings are derived. Our surroundings are occupied; in relation to their occupation, they are doing the reading. We are very careful, occupied by our surrounds. There isn't a set of comfortable seats, which has a clear meaning. We will live for a very long time, we will not read the books. What kind of people destroy books? We don't have time to read the reused materials of ourselves. What kind of people touch plasticine objects? I have been turned into a woman; a woman is our happy issue. We move from the situation to some contexts, represented by 20,000 books that you may not read in the bath. In the path of duty, people feel able to touch me. Do not read the books. I am not as valuable, with parts duly connected, with formerly circumstance. In relation to our surroundings, for the time being, we buy oranges, grapes, and cheap flowers. We represent politically good artworks. We do not represent the good world. The ghost audience reads 20,000 books in the bath, arrives at a consensus: do not touch the plasticine objects. Participating with objects, we try not to be so easy to represent. The plasticine objects look like they want to be touched; we make a living in the bad world, we maintain life. Separated from its context, destruction as a legitimate aim for artists. The artwork is said by native authorities to imply disease, extinction, ornament; I blame myself.

Do not touch the plasticine objects. I feel better about objects by feeling worse about humans. We move from the outside of the art gallery to the inside of the art gallery to the outside of the art gallery. Water descends; fogs and vapours are drawn upwards by the rays of the sun. What kind of people move from the outside to the inside to the outside in order to destroy books? What kind of people read books? Collaborating with objects, we are drawn upwards. We feel bad about feeling bad about feeling bad about the presence of others. We speak quietly. The horizon of humans as the horizon of objects, we act like ourselves, we act like our kindred. The question is about the seasonableness of soft toys, which is a question of resources. The question is about the viability of books, which is a question of good order in a white room. We recognise each other, our political subjectivities; suspicion attaches to our bodies, our bodies speak in a quiet room. We affirm our bodies all the time; we maintain bad politics. 20,000 books say: 'Let's dematerialise.' The books feel entitled to be in the white room. The objects are the limits of our bad politics; we refuse to take responsibility for the objects that cannot exist independently. Do not mention the thing by name, the difficulties of living in a forest. We take our places as the enunciation of a topic. We will not stay for very long. Specialness comes from ubiquity, we will feel ashamed for a very long time. Comfort as a formal circumstance; preservation as the disciplined connection between our parts. We go the last way, in which we ask ourselves: are you doing the reading? Are you watching me doing the reading? Where are you going to die?

Following the Event

* KCL Picket: Pension and Pay Strikes (The Strand, 26th February) * Bread & Roses for All, and Hormones Too (St John on Bethnal Green, 27th February) * March for Education: Pension and Pay Strikes (Bedford Square-Westminster, 28th February) * Women's Strike (Russell Square, 8th March) * Solidarity with Yarl's Wood Hunger Strikers (Home Office, 8th March 2018) *

*

desperate to think and to apprehend
parts of communities that follow the protest
which parts and why they walk in clouds
   of yellow smoke   it matters the smoke
comes from a can   it matters the future
insecure particles of communities
does impartial matter do these empty seats
   we plan to meet   making similarities

relative to our pickets   relation is made up
   all of the struggles in the world   we message
each other small and big struggles
we plan to meet on the street
   even the smallest   there is no loneliness
      like the loneliness follows a sunset
we shouldn't forget a single one of them
solidity is freedom from empty

small and big spaces completely filled up
the property these women's bodies dissuade
   workers from entering arms linking arms
hands on hips signal   unsatisfied
   desires alone women signalling no
go nowhere while we're cooking
we're claiming you're at home
in me   you've got the better of me

making invisible rationalisation of work
we're exclusive as home is from work
work home   we're dependent
  as aloneness to completion

ugly goddess rises from beautiful bodies
still-burning bodies unapprehended
'in numberless roses   and rest shines'
all   men   look   she clouds the sacrifice

we cross the street to meet our friends
every particle in sympathetic relation
      with every other particle   our only property
linked arms let me away with too much
let me take too much   late to the present
kept   secret   the speakers look up to the sky
is a flowering bud isolated from tree
kept secret the blockade so formed

arms not connected with anything else
      speakers direct their oneness upwards
      exposing the evening sky to risk
dissolution struck through with sorrow
happiness depends upon continuity if
we look like a solid or unbroken mass
if   we satisfy desires without labour
a single one of us bodies assertion

*

being at many not desirous forever
in   the   pub   that   follows   the   picket
the next night settles immediately
      our deep divisions flow into the sky
no time for 'light and air'   we can
'love and sorrow' after the event
dissolution as the absence of difference
not tonight 'my heart desires too much'

every body projecting onto every other
      body   we're afraid of losing ourselves
demand bodily autonomy access to healthcare
reproductive justice   what have we got
to lose directly in service of shatter
'*expression after the shatter*
of these hierarchies'   mirror
      invisible the limits of family love

will my own self will disappear
discontinuities of care   some   demand
some relation no longer relation
how can we help and who can we ask
don't look   accept good collaboration
   admit your obsolescence   unblock
every opening abandoning property
smoke out your own   occupying space

if you must stay you have dependents
   name your signifying   infinite your signature
beat spirit with wings   rise for the duration
   of the event   petition widespread consent
drift upon specifics how much by when
the form would be better not end after name
prepare your defences   you are not at risk
separate lighter particles blow them away

belch the purple clouds out of your body
go over your argument call in your favours
stand in your power 'come, you spirits
   that tend on mortal thoughts' 'come, thick night'
you are frown-born smoke-gendered
end-willed 'directly in contact with
everything possible' no longer the enemy
remembering 'you can have what you ask for,

*

ask for / everything'   remember you can
refuse to wait and wait refuse to work
and work   by virtue of your witch's
breasts your idle hands unsexing life
will your own future will disappear
the commutation of sympathy for fear
sister on sister determined by mirrors
put down by their bodies exposed to   male

violence   exposing their wounds   weapons
repressive empowerment their busy hands
femininity modelled on making us similar
making everyday acts of bad nature
acts of good citizenship pink sociality
   legislated   and   enforced
we avoid pursing our lips making fun
of pursed lips   the international division

of labour lengthens the working day
her legs spread the limits set by the sun
      we share the same enemies
our sympathies the limits set by our enemies
to instrumentalise these pronouns
to valorise these shifts these vaster fields of view
let's stop suffering correspondence
while we were drifting in and out

of rhetorical positions talking about
dancing all night when we were young
last weekend   she's reported drifting smoke
meaning resides in the attempt to be close
particles don't lose themselves just like that
      strike for solidarity signal across the street
we will drive our bodies into the ground
      commuting soil for spirit for soil

*

for the lowest and highest possible knowledge
'the enlightened and unenlightened   will   shake
   hands' will pull spirit down from sky
we stand upon spirit handholding pitchforks
ugly goddess sets bright stars to fall
into disuse solid black clouds sustain
us as well as anonymous charges
impartial mechanisms of absence of light

*

restraints may be undetermined   brown
and black arms wave from partially opened
windows   to hear with the arms to see with
the legs   kicking foretelling shut it down communicable
to the uninitiated   spreading beyond
       the bounds of propriety we sing outside
the home office   our petitions for freedom
shatter the illusion of freedom   signing

our names to the charge that 'everything
beyond a spreadsheet is a mystery to them'
we destroy the whole world   the great
spreadsheet   after the event after the dissolution
       of spirit   we level disenchantment
starting again from the ground   contemptuous
not   for   forever   songs fade away contemptuous
not for continuities   we message each other

*

we   plan   to   meet

Futures Flowers

You want to imagine futures. You want to create futures' objects in your mind and to hold them there, until your mind turns into the shapes of these objects. The practice of imagining turns into the rightness of action, according to the metaphysics of the ritual, so that flowers formed by the hands become the fruits of the practice become abolition's efflorescence. The ritual must be repeated until it turns on itself, its objects destroying their causality. You turn on yourself, move into the void in yourself, and begin...

The red door to the temple is guarded by two elephants, both vomiting rainbows. Their vomit meets in the sky above them and fuses to form a lunette. The lunette is decorated with brides-to-be standing a corpse-width apart. One is to be enjoyed; one worshipped only. The brides are protected by lions, who are nothing like the real police sitting across the street from the real temple. They protect and enforce the reality that requires them; you do not require them.

You prefer these lions who prop open their mouths with the heads of your enemies. You decide to substitute yourself for your enemies, abolishing liberalism by means of liberalism, placing your head in the lion's mouth. Lying between the brides you realise that your body is corpse-width; yours is the corpse by which you must enter.

Past the first hurdle, you throw coloured powders at the space where the door should be, trying to make it appear in your mind. It's a jewelled throne on an island of butter in the ocean of milk. It's a forest of the lotus of the heart that abides in the citadel. It's a red door to a temple in the cremation ground inside your body. Mind guards the door to consciousness.

The coloured powders fall into a geometric pattern on the ground of being and nonbeing. You lie down and puff your way in – it's easy! – you make it all the way, breaking through three straight lines, discontinuing tenses. Blow time out of mind, let futures flowers...

Another line appears, a dark line formed by a cloud's shadow. The cloud rearranges itself in the sky – it's an elephant, it's your mind stuck in mind – the dark line marks its time of death. The elephant bursts into hundreds of thousands of silvery spheres. You stand in the shadows, looking up, mouth wide open in awe of futurity. You swallow spheres, internalise obstacles that you may pass them through your body. Pass memories of elephants, pass clouds.

The line increases and covers ground; it's the side of a circle, accounting for error. The circumference is planted with golden arms, reaching upwards, stretching to hold each other's hands at the apex. You know there are no multicoloured hands across the world; there are oceans of wine surrounding mountains of flesh. Nevertheless, you visualise a circle of arms raising a cone of power, vitriol crystallising into bluestone. True solidarity is a beautiful and charmingly corrosive process. What if the future is faceless?

Return to the shadows. You project your shadows onto the clouds, casting your self-esteem, all those little mothers, into outer space. Mind-rays alight! Little mothers carry lamps out of your body and up to the stars. Infatuated with darkness, you resist their advice: 'Luminosity is the state of things that are luminous and also of things that are dark.'

You want to be left alone with your mind-rays, a cosmic puppet, dangling in the grandeur of the inner void, your desirelessness. But you are surrounded by kissy noises, resonating concentrically. Everyone and everything is kissing, except you! Your mouth is stuffed full of flowers and even these flowers are kissing each other, inside your mouth as if you were simply a space in which desire takes place. You struggle to imagine kissing from the perspective of your mouth. Your tongue is a brazen plate struck by lightning, and struck, and struck. You know that subtle sounds are better, unstruck sounds are best, and bite down on your tongue.

You bite off the head of your enemy and join in with anticipation. The cracks in the walls of the temple are stuffed with little yellow chrysanthemums. You remove these flowers and destabilise the temple in your race to one-pointed consciousness, which is the brain-facing lotus at the crown of your skull. The crown hides a hole, into which sky drips, feeding the thousand-petalled lotus that blooms behind and occasionally into and out of your eyes, your ears, your mouth. Feel the petals tickle your mind when you shake your head out of time. Feel the roots of the lotus penetrate the wet soil of sky and spread into the infinite wetness of space. No, not yet; the temple stands.

You must grasp the triangles, for one who is not a triangle must not worship triangles. The lines and angles suggest hundreds of thousands of awkward bodies, golden arms, sword-fighting, sunbeams, laser quests, illuminated parts. But you strive for unbroken light, sectionless consciousness, sparkling waves of bliss.

The triangles exist in another dimension. They cast shadows in the shape of cubes in the shape of spheres, cast these shadows upon your body, cover your body in perfect solids. How absurd, the masters say, to spread perfection on your body like jam on bread. But you delight in hyperreality, this calculated immersion in pleasure, you pass yourself through your body without breaking your body, you make your shadows dance.

Your shadows hold hands, rub beaks, play footsie, wind tails together, totter rosily, cheek to cheek, bumpity bump bump bump. They circle each other, full-body bobbing; they take each other by surprise, stand to attention, and star-gaze. The absolute soul of the universe is an assemblage of migratory birds, whose agitation is indeed creation. You understand that when they say they dream to change the world, what they really mean is that they sleep badly. You say something about sleeping badly: 'the death of death whose destruction is liberation'. You say nothing about the seeds in your heart, the roots creeping into your circulatory system, the seedlings poking out of your centre of consciousness.

In truth, your desires are infinite, your actions infinitesimal. You are as close as you can get to the centre before sneezing, the temple inside you implodes in a mess of cremation ash, yellow pollen, third-eye twinkle, and sonic dot. You are as far away as you can get from the world without renouncing it. Opposing yourself, you do all this as an offering to me, these flowers formed by the hands, this worship through the flesh, these lightning flashes of social life, this rhythm through rightness and opposition. You turn out of these objects, turning out.

Villein in Gross

The villain is one who rents space in her mind: there will always be a place for you, whether I want it or not. There will always be a circle drawn in white chalk, a place to sit and work in the hunting grounds.

The past actually happened, which is the present reality of your access to these grounds. One who offers to hide the birds and keep them safe in her mouth.

The duck and the goose and the flamingo, some of them fine, all of them wanting in fineness. For shitting in the garden is neither good nor bad, but gardening makes it so.

In her attempts to identify with the dream of the commons, she overidentifies with the object of the critique's critique. She is deeply involved in the commission of disgraceful crimes: inserting the skeleton of a small, common bird inside the skeleton of a big, common bird.

I would invest in the realisation of the commons were it not that I have gross dreams: puppy-loving, shit-claiming, full-timing, full-ownership. One who swallows small and big bones.

Villainous or base service means being bonded to the family, not the family home. One who is welcome to clean, not to use, the toilet.

To me, it is a prison, I never reach it in time. The desire to be timely, my shadow's shadow. It is the kind of ambition that you would describe as 'swallowing large fruit'. It is the kind of fruit that you would blame for being 'full of pulp, large and succulent'.

A monstrous fruit, full of bad seeds, like the small bodies of goldcrest wrens inside the big body of a cockroach. She pays to crush seeds.

Inheritance is a perishable body, sustained by food. A bowl of rice, in which there are many confines, wards, and dungeons. Rice's power of disposal is more or less limited by custom, the nameless dread of the dinner party. One who spits after eating.

A soiled table cloth, which invests the gross body, which invests the soul. It is thrice-framed like a sheath of repulsion in a sheath of protective custody in a sheath of affective debt. A bloodshot eyeball in a brown eggshell in a silkworm's cocoon. A rustic loaf of bread in a verbal contract in a comfortable family home.

One who breaks the circle, as if the grounds of inheritance never actually happened.

No comfort blankets, no enclosures, no borders. One whose flesh, bone, marrow, blood, fat, faeces, urine leave her body unambiguously.

A monstrous disposition, bound to looking back over the shoulder. A preoccupation with the past that is liable to be corrupted unless broken up into many small and big occupations and corrupted, one by one.

Villein Regardant

The villain is one who rents space outside her body, inside a forest. She can barely tell the difference between the big inside and outside of the forest and reality, and the small insides and outsides of the forest's realities, but the forest assures her that the difference is there to protect her.

Trained to believe that she has a manifest destiny to rent, a duty not to own, she sits and works on the inside in order to sit and work at all.

Inside the forest is a ghost town; the space is populated by voices without culpability, violent imagery without hermeneutic limits. One who is paid to set limits inside the seminar room that she knows to be unreal.

Imagine an ivory tower without windows, a forest without breaks in its canopy. Imagine the manifestations of dying and death at the centre, the reproduction of ghosts necessary to protect the establishment of the ghost town.

Imagine the lights that come to light at this kind of centre, where ideas may be grasped by the hands. The forest is infested with these kinds of lights, trained upon ideas that must make exhibitions of themselves, that must be handled by customs to be grasped.

Shoulders back, she walks into the opening between manifesto and manifest, to demonstrate her point about point's void. She knows not to look back over the shoulder as she walks, for people might make an example of her, and it is she who must disappear.

For example, one who looks back over the shoulder when walking in and out of doors, and disappears, when walking up and down stairs, and disappears, when walking in and out of rooms, and disappears, when walking up and down corridors, and disappears.

Whispers are bound to the institution. Everyone knows which doors to stay away from; not everyone knows. Didn't anyone tell you not to walk up and down those stairs; no one told me. Everyone knows which rooms to avoid; not everyone knows. Didn't anyone warn you about those corridors; no one warned me. Whisperers bear the marks of their disclosures.

We are the ones who must share these warnings. Step into the negative spaces between circles, the breaks between cliques. Rub up against becoming networks in these kinds of breaks, agitate for spaces as breaks.

Renounce the kind of protection afforded by the forest, the rationale of duty, the kind of safety afforded by ghosts, the duty of rationale.

Imagine boundless pleasures. Imagine break without point.

Bibliography

Ahmed, Sara, *On Being Included: Racism and Diversity in Institutional Life* (Durham: Duke University Press, 2012)

Clément, Catherine, *Syncope: The Philosophy of Rapture*, translated by Sally O'Driscoll and Deirdre M. Mahoney (Minneapolis: University of Minnesota, 1994)

di Prima, Diane, 'Revolutionary Letter #19', *Revolutionary Letters* (San Francisco: City Lights Books, 1974)

Fanon, Frantz, *Black Skin, White Masks*, translated by Charles Lam Markmann (London: Pluto Press, 2008)

Federici, Silvia, *Caliban and the Witch: Women, the Body and Primitive Accumulation* (Brooklyn, New York; Autonomedia, 2014)

Glissant, Édouard,
– *Poetics of Relation*, translated by Betsy Wing (Ann Arbor: University of Michigan Press, 2010)
– Manthia Diawara, 'Conversation with Édouard Glissant Aboard the Queen Mary II', translated by Christopher Winks (August 2009)

Hegel, Georg Wilhelm Friedrich, 'First System – Programme of German Idealism' (1796), translated by Edmund Hardy ([unpublished], 2010)

Hölderlin, Friedrich, 'Evening Fantasy' (1799), translated by Edmund Hardy ([unpublished], 2018)

Monier-Williams, *A Sanskrit-English Dictionary: Etymologically and Philologically Arranged with Special Reference to Cognate Indo-European Languages* (New Delhi: Asian Educational Services, 2008)

Padoux, André, and Jeanty, Roger-Orphé, *The Heart of the Yoginī: The Yoginīhṛdaya, a Sanskrit Tantric Treatise* (Oxford: Oxford University Press, 2013)

Radhakrishnan, S., *The Principal Upaniṣads* (New Delhi: Oxford University Press, 1989)

Raha, Nat, 'Future Justice in the Present', *Radical Transfeminism* (Leith, Scotland: Sociopathetic Distro, 2017)

Woodroffe, John, *Shakti and Shakta: Essays and Addresses on the Shakta Tantrashastra* (Charleston: BiblioBazaar, 2008)

Uziell, Laurel, 'untitled', *ZARF*, No. 3 (Spring 2016)

Acknowledgments

'Containing Passages from Dictionaries; Along with the Shell or Husk; Along with the Membrane': This poem was first published in *Visual Verse* (November 2013), with thanks to Preti Taneja, radiating literary disrupter and the first editor to support my work. Thank you to Amy Pettifer and Jennifer Boyd for commissioning an audio recording of this poem for SHELL LIKE (October 2017) and revivifying it (after Leonora Carrington's 'The Happy Corpse') in live, online, and print contexts.

'stupid, a kind of bracelet': This poem was first published in *Jungftak: A Journal for Prose-Poetry* (April 2015), with thanks to Eley Williams, whose thumbed oranges, wishful seeds, and enclitical clusters have made this world marvellous, and other delphinestrian, or, scamble-shambling things.

'Awkward Bumping in the Theory District': The title is a reference to 'hand up to your ear' by Fred Moten and 'Metalipsis for Uyen Hua' by Joshua Clover. This poem was first published in *Ambit* (Spring 2016), with thanks to Ralf Webb. Thank you to Megan Zword for reviewing it in *Hix Eros* (August 2016).

'Secretions and Obstructions': This poem was written after conversations with Nat Raha, Dorothy Wang, and Sam Solomon, and the first year of co-organising 'Race & Poetry & Poetics in the UK' (2015-2016), for which I will never stop being grateful. Thank you to Laurel Uziell for allowing me to quote their poem (and for sneaking tinnies into the Forward Prizes). This poem was first published in *Litmus Magazine* (November 2016), with thanks to Dorothy Lehane, and then in *The Forward Book of Poetry 2018* , with thanks to the judges for highly commending it.

'Responses to a Question about Citation': Thank you to my mother for growing such beautiful flowers, and for trying (and failing) to teach us their names. This poem was written specially so that I could submit something to Callie Gardner for *Zarf* and was first published in *Zarf* (February 2017), with thanks to Callie.

'Thank You Poem for Robert Hampson': This poem was first published in *For Robert: An Anthology* (June 2017), which was compiled by Redell Olsen on the occasion of Robert's retirement from Royal Holloway. Thank you to my extraordinary teachers – Dell, Robert, Kristen Kreider, Will Montgomery, and Jo Shapcott – to whom I perform site-specific remediations of the ritual salutations. Thank you to Karen Sandhu, Ryan Ormonde, Sejal Chad, and Prudence Bussey-Chamberlain, for making Poetic Practice as personally transformative as it was otherwise transformative.

Review of Hannah Black's *Some Context* : Thank you to Robert Kiely for accompanying me to the exhibition, asking and inciting so many questions, and breaking and unbreaking so many rules. This review was first published in *MAP* (October 2017), with thanks to Daisy Lafarge.

'Following the Event': Thank you to Edmund Hardy and Nat for allowing me to quote their work. Thank you to the friends and people I don't know who put in so much un(der)paid labour to organise the events, to the poets who wrote and read strike poems on and beyond the picket, to Špela Drnovšek Zorko, Emilia Weber, Tom Betteridge, Holly Pester, Derawan Rahmantavy, James Goodwin, and friends named elsewhere in these acknowledgements. This poem was first performed at 'Suffrage in Bloomsbury: Writing Women in Bedford Square' (London, March 2018), with thanks to Dell, and then published in *Spells: 21*st *Century Occult Poetry* (2018), with thanks to Sarah Shin and Rebecca Tamás.

'Futures Flowers': Some of the real temples in this poem are in Hyderabad; thank you to my family for going along with me, always. Thank you to Eley for introducing Generative Constraints to videos of albatrosses courting, to Generative Constraints for realising the multi-scalar significance of this courtship, and to Edmund & Benjamin Thompson for introducing me to the Numberphile channel on YouTube. This poem was first performed at Hard To Get's 'An Aspirin the Size of the Sun' (Oxford, May 2018), with thanks to Grace Linden and Gazelle Mba, and then published in *Chicago Review* (Winter 2018-2019), with thanks to the editors. Thank you to Isabel Waidner for weaponizing the vomit hearts in the cause of our diamond stuff.

'Villein in Gross' & 'Villein Regardant': These poems were first performed, respectively, at 'An A-Z of Villainy' (London, May 2018), with thanks to Kate Potts, and 'Public Feeling, Dissident Acts: Dismantling Cultures of Sexual Harassment in Universities' (London, June 2018), with thanks to Lisa Blackman. They were then published in *Cambridge Literary Review* (2018), with thanks to Lydia Wilson and Rosie Šnajdr.

Milton Keynes UK
Ingram Content Group UK Ltd.
UKHW051017210624
444394UK00008B/103

9 781912 802289